Lullabies for

a Goat-born Lady

Lovelines for

a Goat-born Lady

JOHN AGARD

SERPENT'S
TAIL

Library of Congress Catalog Card Number: 90-60288

British Library Cataloguing in Publication Data
Agard, John, *1949 –*
   Lovelines for a goat-born lady.
   I. Title
   811

ISBN 1-85242-201-7

First published 1990 by
Serpent's Tail, 4 Blackstock Mews, London N4

Typeset in 10/13pt Plantin by AKM Associates (UK) Ltd, London

Printed in Great Britain by
The Longdunn Press, Bristol

for Grace

Contents

Blueback Memory

Goat-born Lady

Beloved capricorn
      my goat-born lady
           gracing the horn of plenty

Shall I play the goat
in the hill of your armpit
or do you prefer me
to climb towards your cleft?

Go Spread Wings

If I be the rain
you the earth
let love be the seed
and together
make we give birth
to a new longing
for harmony growing
among all things
and love go spread wings
love go spread wings

If I be a tree
clinging to parch earth
this time you be the rain
and love the wind
taking we by the hand
showing the way
to new awakenings
and love go spread wings
love go spread wings

Mudhead Woman*

Mudhead woman
from a hot land.
Sunperson at heart
despite hayfever.
One whose spirit
gets weighed down
by dim bulbs in curtained rooms
of dis england.
You like to see fire
glow in a grate.

Mudhead woman
in a cold land.
Kiskadee music
still play in yuh head
though you make
bluetit acquaintance,
and when you dance
a georgetown breeze
move in yuh waist.

Mudhead woman
still linked to yuh mother
by a fried plantain love.
Lemme give you a foreday morning hug
under dis quilt of england.

*Mudhead – a fond expression applied to Guyanese
because of Guyana's low-lying silty coastland

By All Means Bless

By all means
bless the cloth
that wiped
the face
of Jesus

By all means
bless the towel
that unfolds
an infant
like miraculous bread

By all means
bless the towel
the boxer returns to
– a brief harbour
after a harassing round

By all means
bless the sacred silk
that garbs
the sumo's
amplitude of loin

But I say this also
bless the towel
that unwraps
your buttocks
(fresh out of the shower)
with such casual ease

we overlook
life's small epiphanies

Somewhere

Somewhere in her body
there must be a hidden forest.
Somewhere in this forest
there must be a hidden bush.
Somewhere in this bush
there must be a hidden creek.
Somewhere in this creek
there must be hidden wealth.
But I have not come to speak of diamonds.
I have merely come to bathe my mouth
and taste the secret of her water.

No Ordinary Thing

Small days walk on stilts.
Mother Sally dances in your childhood eye.
Masquerade magic rivets you to a window,
eyes wide enough to accommodate a ritual,
and what the drum doing to you
will not be mentioned in your passport.

Small days get high on fruit.
Your young mouth dismembers a starapple
that stains lips with innocent semen.
I conjure you, little red girl
back in a tropical time,
willing your own nipples into bud.
Rudeness is part of your heritage.
Your mother, playing the piano,
scolds you for repeating a brazen folksong.
You discover geography between your legs
but go to bed with Enid Blyton.

Now wrap a warm scarf around your neck
and think of the tropical riddles that reside
beneath your winter coat.

No ordinary thing, my love.

Circles

Mud is transformed by hopscotch circles of light.
Your little girl legs flounce free as rain.
You redesign creation in small hops.

Now let's hopscotch back into the first garden.
Let's invite the serpent to our circle.
Let's share an apple with a touch of salt.

Yu De Headmaster Daughter

So yu bathe
yu bathe yu skin
in river water
yu de headmaster daughter

So yu raid
yu raid yu neighbour
guenip tree
an feast yu mouth
pon coconut growee
yu de headmaster daughter

So yu fraid
yu fraid cockroach flight
but find candlefly light
mysterious news
yu de headmaster daughter

So yu lose
yu lose yuself
in de gift of fish
        reflection
not far from yu doorstep
yu de headmaster daughter

I wonder what de headmaster
would say now
to see dis blossom-out poetwoman
walking in the ways of she vision

bearing she father eyes
reclaiming she mother wings

More Than a Habit

Miss Curling Toes
she can't help it.
Curling she toes
is more than a habit,
curling she toes
is she nature,
curling she toes
is she feature.
Miss Curling toes
curl dem toes fuh me
curl dem like little sea-creature.

O ten little prophets
of private pleasure.

Blueback Memory

Tell de blueback crab
wid midnight on he back
tell de blueback crab for me
dat if yu see how Gracey
a-stroll under horsechestnut tree
but she still hold yu waving tengeleh
in de basket of she memory

Tell de blueback crab
wid midnight on he back
tell de blueback crab for me
dat Gracey send howdee
and ask one small favour.
Sign she name in shining mud
sign it in midnight blue
and she in turn my blueback friend
will crush one autumn leaf for you

Unnoticed

In your tuft of light
I am a gleaming lizard
come out of the shadow of myself
to discover myself anew
on the trembling branch of your body.

Let us lie still.
Let us aspire to the camouflaging
art of coupling lizards
that time may slip us by. Unnoticed.

Hayfever Affair

Pollen is a ruthless lover
that plunders her sense of sun
ravishing her nostrils with itches
brimming her eyes with redness
streaming her cheeks with sneezes

Pollen – slick one
                    on a bastard breeze –
you pollinate my woman with discomfort

we don't need you for a threesome

Traveller

I have entered
the house
of your body
on burning feet

I have lain
my shoes
by the doorway
of your welcome

I who have carried
my pain
like a drum
through winding streets
of the skull

and wandered
through puddles
of flesh
where one's shadow
turns to ashes

now wipe
the crossroads
from my skin

and under the roof
of your shaping hands
replenish my steps

When Images Fail

Sometimes
I imagine you
a tree
growing out of me
your branches
doing some mysterious naked dance

sometimes
I imagine you
a river
flowing over me
longlost secrets
of ancestral presence

but then
when images fail
and the tongue
stumbles
in love's blinding flame

I merely call your name
noting how
we take our blessings for granted

In Times of Love

In times of love
simple things spring new life
ancient patterns weave
fresh meanings
to your fevered eyes

the sun
you never looked for in the skies
offers your skin
a flaming benediction
and the rain
once a nuisance to your day
is living drum
for warming blood
and twinning flesh

in times of love
you let the child inside of us
have its way
and learn to look for dreams
beneath the dust

It Made No Difference

The river leaned closer
her dimpled cheeks
for the caressing
fingertips of sunlight

it made no difference
that her effulgent face
was murked with oil

it made no difference
that the scavenger crows
were standing by
in capes of mourning

just then i watched you
touched by nature's loveplay
peel your shoes
and wade calfdeep
in ripples blushing sunlight

Now

Face up
to the browning of the sun

we laze
in heaven's blue eye

while a chirping kiskadee
interprets for us
the colour of silence

Lovepoem Slowly Turning Into a Lullaby

Starapple of my eye
my firefly in pitchdense of night.
Sleep tight on the drift of your dreams.
This is a lovepoem slowly turning into a lullaby

My salt and pepper
when ole higue shedding sly skin,
my wide sheet over mirror
when lightning scrawling sky.
Sleep tight on the drift of your dreams.
This is a lovepoem slowly turning into a lullaby.

Lucky seed in my palm of hope,
my heavensent in hard guava season.
Sleep tight on the drift of your dreams.
This is a lovepoem slowly turning into a lullaby.

My white rum whisperings
from the corner of my heart,
my good breeze tidings
to so many unanswerable whys.
Sleep tight on the drift of your dreams.
This is a lovepoem slowly turning into a lullaby.

Interlude & Elements (or I'll be back in a second)

A small waterfall –
a homely rain –
little fountain murmuring –

that sound
of your woman peeing
behind a half-closed door

now she is back in bed
relieved of her running water
but bursting with fire

stay awake pink-eyed one
not yet the air of dreams

for you your woman and the gods
have some unfinished business
                    of earth

Moonbelly
(*a pregnancy sequence*)

1

Your belly can no longer be anonymous
even in full-blown blouse.
Pregnancy is now your landscape
and fullness comes to claim your shape.

2
Drumseed
        a-bloom
wit de speed
        of water

daddywater
        meet
mammywater
        in one twinkling

monthly blood
turn back
it own tide

monthly blood
have new mouth
to feed

an new mouth is new bud

When mammywater
an daddywater
meet

Wit god blessing
spirits willing

        navel string
            soon sing

3

It is a globe –
your belly big with child.
Granted you cannot spin it
to trace a country with a finger,
but it is a globe.

On its still axis
unmapped waters turn
a world coming into view
by loving degrees.
A continent is happening.

Your belly big with child
is geography made new,
and your navel the centre
from which all marvels
take their bearings.

4

Moonbelly
moonbelly
mind how yu go

moonbelly
moonbelly
take it slow

moonbelly
moonbelly
go carefully
among the hurrying crowds

remember
elbows have edges
and pointed umbrellas
think they own the world

moonbelly
moonbelly
mind how yu go

moonbelly
moonbelly
take it slow

5

I will miss
that brown moon
rising over your pubic crest
eclipsing your knickers' nylon horizon

When your belly reclaims its flatness,
I will miss watching you stand
in the bloom of your own reflection.

The Lover

What can i do

when he weaves
his spell
of softness
over you

what can i do

when his gentle
fingers touch
your eyes
like leaves

what can i do

when your cheeks
glow peace
and you weaken
in his presence

what can i do

when you open
to the lover
by the name
of sleep

On the Waters

Asleep, your body is a ship
bound for dreamland.
I come into bed like a stowaway.

Adrift, on the waters of contradiction
who can tell ship from water
stowaway from dreamer?

Blessed Undressed

Blessed you
are undressed.
Blessed undressed.
Obsessed I
for you undressed
will find no rest
till I obsessed
am blessed
by you undressed
and you obsessed
are blessed
by me undressed.
These tongue-twisting words
will put us through
time's tongue-twisting test
till no more no less
no worst no best
no me no you.

Just two creatures
rooting in the soil of heaven.
Blessed, undressed, at rest.

Other Mouth

The mouth the world sees
the mouth you eat with
the mouth you speak with
the mouth you use to voice a poem
the mouth you use to rejoice in song
the mouth you use to be simply social
the mouth basking in its own smile
the mouth that yawns and answers the phone
the mouth exposed to the four directions

But what about the other mouth?
The mouth the world does not see
the mouth you throb with
the mouth you tide with
the mouth you use to earth a cock
the mouth you use to birth a child
the mouth basking in its own wetness
the mouth that flames without fire
the mouth at which the four directions become one

Mirrors

Switching from dress to dress
you face the truth of mirrors
with your woman's dream
and fragile human need
to stun the staring world

but when the face of mirrors
tells you that they lie
and the world's fault-finding eye
does not see your private hurt

you will turn to find in me
a human mirror
for the hidden self
that others fail to hold or see

Ode to Knickers

O red knickers
robe her in fire

O yellow knickers
grace her in sunflower

O black knickers
lace her in nightriddle

O blue knickers
sheen her in searipple

O green knickers
frill her in wetness of leaf

O white knickers
fringe her in maidenmilk

O knickers all
whatever your colour
flimsy container of wonder

receiving no word of thanks
yet offering awkward hands

   to ponder

Lead Me

Lead me to your wanton parts
that I may graze
with holy glee.

Four-footed buddhas chew their cud
and every blade of grass
is a common gift
for eyes to see.

And I ambitious man,
who learns to stand upright,
must learn again to bend
towards the light.

O the grass is singing
between the legs of you and me
and milk gathers
like a drop of truth

Invocation

Lord of iron, Ogun,
grant me hardness
when and where it matters

Queen of waters, Yemanja,
bless my man-water
with good seed

Sacred harlot, Oshun,
bejewelled to the crotch
girdled with the moon
guide me to the slut
beneath my graceful lady

Sky-Serpent, Damballah,
may I inherit
your divine wriggle
when I lie on her

You there, Legba,
randy trickster,
keeper of the gateway
guardian of the centrepiece,
help me transfix her

While governments making plans
your vulva sparkles on my moustache
we guilty of a subversive trickle

Rituals

There are rituals waiting to be kissed
from under your skin.
already the water spirits gather
at your secret openings
and news has reached your toes

What need for sacrificial chicken or goat
when time wields a commonplace knife
and lovers offer a radiant throat

2

tonight as usual you plait your hair
legs curled beneath you on a sofa
doing to your head what is done to bread
feeding the multitude of your dreams
where the comb cannot reach

3

and in some corner of ancestral memory
she walking a land where men pan for gold
skin washed in creeks the colour of coffee
she cupping a black pearl between she legs
and only the silk cotton tree know her secret

and in some corner of ancestral fantasy
she taking the road that lead to possession
because she want the gods to ride she waist
and her pores speak with gift of tongues
forgetting a good methodist upbringing

4
but tonight no breaking of egg no scattering of rice
tonight you simply pull the curtain closer
throw a dressing gown over a chair
turn off the light and come into bed

these small rituals bind us to tenderness
but there are beasts waiting to be fed

Small Thought

The past sits like a fatalist
in the throne of your eyes
weighing the blows of time
questioning the greenery of gifts.
I console myself with a small thought
– that in legends as in life
thrones can be toppled by a kiss

Just Once

Just once before you sleep
the sleep of rivers
after rage of fired flesh

just once just once again
before you sleep the sleep of rivers
and the dog of time sniffs out our trail
let's hold each other close as rain
dreaming the dream of mountains

Creole Romance

Wind and River Romance

Wind forever playing loverboy
bringing he breezy joy
to everything he touch
but Wind you can't trust

Forever playing fresh
with big woman like me
He forget I name River –
passing he hand over me face
tickling me bellyskin
talking to me in whisper

Promising to bring down
the moon and the stars
and lay them in me lap
even when hot sun shining
but sweet whispering don't catch me

I know Wind too good
I does just flow along to faithful Sea
and let Wind sweet words pass by
like cool breeze

Antillean Breeze

Coconut trees
returning the caress
of antillean breeze
and two human beings
up to their knees
in love

Sea
is an ancient rhythm
in the seat of the spine
but sea marked
with footprints
of blood like wine

Before conquistador
or fatal ship
trailing a terrible passage
two human beings
make room for each other
outside the confine
of any language

Up to their knees
in antillean breeze
they ravish the myth of love

On a Morning Like This

Morning unwrapping her skirt of mist
like a brazen ghost

Dasheen leaf done trap quicksilver drop
of nightbefore rain

Sunrise over zinc roof is a holy host
in a priestly sky

On a morning like this it is time
to bruise your lips
on forbidden fruit

On a morning like this it is time
to stand outside your door
and count yourself poor

when you have no one to kiss

Kissing Rocks

Kissing Rocks
they call you –
two massive rocks
clinching foreheads
on Mabaruma's
green hip of land

weighted
on steep earth
mated
in mid-poise
you two lovebird rocks

your solid intimacy
undisturbed by centuries
linger longer
than the crash of fallen trees

Watermelon Lady

Watermelon Lady
I really thirsty
and I like wha I see
Watermelon lady
cool this thirst for me

Watermelon lady
I can't wait to sink
meh mouth in dem pink
half-moon-o-sweetness
in you hand

Watermelon lady
only you could cool
this thirst man

Watermelon lady
you got you face
so serious
but when I look down at you tray
is luscious
pink lips smiling away

Watermelon lady
I go faint in the sunshine
if you don't cool
this thirst of mine

Watermelon lady
you have me hanging on so long
you think that is nice?
I dying for a slice

this sun ain't fun
this sun ain't fun

Bouncy Bella

Bouncy Bella a-paddle de boat
Bouncy Bella a-milk de goat

Bouncy Bella a-fork up de land
Bouncy Bella a-fetch in de sand

Bouncy Bella a-fix fowl pen
Bouncy Bella a-feed de hen

Bouncy Bella a-weed de yard
Bouncy Bella a-work so hard

Village a-talk say Bouncy Bella
Married to one lazy lazy fella

Bouncy Bella say yes he lazy
but between he foot he frisky

Crab-boy

Crab-boy
Crab-boy
dancing sideways on moonlight track

Crab-boy
Crab-boy
velvet blue night shine on yuh back

Crab-boy
Crab-boy
foolish Crab-boy
carrying basket to fetch water

Crab-boy
Crab-boy
mannish Crab-boy
exposing yuh lo-lo to River-Mama daughter

Jumbie Romance

In a radiant crotch of night
firefly scatter
hieroglyphics over ancient bush
and shadows learn to blush

on a night like this
jumbie does play tricks
and unseen things mix
supernatural fear with lust

forest demons lay a promise
in the fork of your lap
and with sweet talk
blind you to their cloven walk

so mind how you step
over bridge and track
once you see naked jumbie
no turning back

2
From de time I cast me gaze
pon River-Mama bubbie
I know I was doomed to spend me days
under river creek or sea

forever slave to River-Mama
dat woman with heart of fish
now I have to comb and comb de hair
of dat moonlight-laden bitch

but for all the gold I aint miss
my mortal flesh or home
for River-Mama is my water-self
my soul is in she comb

Mek Four

Who seh West Indian creole
is not a language of love?
Well I tell you . . .

When me and she eye
mek four
negative vibration
walk out de door

when me and she eye
mek four
tenderness was a guest
that didn't need invitation

when me and she eye
mek four
the world was neither
more or less
but a moment of rightness

we tongue locked
in a syntax of yes

Utterance

One humming bird morning
woman say to man
   i feel so divine
   i want to feel you wine
    like a eel
   between dis pum-pum of mine

such candour
made grass blush
every insect bristled

and hunger
crawled on all fours

    seeking utterance

She

Wriggle like eel
Sting like honey bee
I like how it feel
When you do dat to me

He

Squeeze me like crab
Scratch like cow itch
God mek sweetness
For de poor and de rich

Old Man's Proposal

Red-pepper gal
why yu na sing fo me?
All night long long yu sing brazen song
but though me ask pon bended knee
yu say yu na sing fo man like me

Red-pepper gal
why yu na dance fo me?
Me hear seh how yu mek yu waist float
softer than water lily in a breeze
but yu say yu na dance fo one stupid old goat

Ah red-pepper gal
me like yu cause yu mouth so hot
me will cross land an sea fo give yu all me got
an if it please yu nature
dis old goat will nyam raw pepper from yuh lap
                                    an call it home

Young Woman's Reply

Me is a sprightly tree
an you want come
                    peel off mih blossom
                    wid yuh john crow eye

Me is a spreading wing
tuned to sky
an you want come
                    limit mih to ground

Me is a winning card
in de game of life
an you want come
                    circle mih luck

But old man you have pluck
an you may yet taste red-pepper
if you have breath enough to meet me
                    mountain top

Between Two

Rain
a-shake
shac-shac
pon housetop
an a man
an woman
a-lay down
back to back

lawd mek dis tension pass
blow way dis grievance
like dry grass

Riddle

HIBISCUS FLY UP TO MIH CHEEK
No that ain't why I turn red
my love guess again guess again

HUMMING BIRD GONE TO MIH PULSE
no that ain't why my blood beat so
guess again my love guess again

GUENIP SEED STICK IN MIH THROAT
no that ain't why I swallow hard
my love guess again guess again

for this thing called heart
is a guessing radiance

and love is a common riddle

Through the Fingers of Time

Old Couple

Sharing silence
like a tangerine
they suck at memories
enjoy the juice of dreams
collect the skins of moments
time did not discard
finding ardour in stillness

Love at First Sight

Their eyes met
when they dropped their contact lenses
into the same bowl of water.

Wedding Ring

Through the fingers of time
a dream glitters and spins
for better or for worse.

Discovery

When my grandmother discovered her clit
she was no longer content just to knit.

The Widow

My little house has not been swept,
not since my husband's death.
But no more mourning for me.
Open up the window, throw away the key.

Ashes to ashes, dust to dust,
but a widow's house needs a little lust.
Sprinkle powder, rub on the perfume,
Come young man, bring your broom.

My little house has not been swept,
not since my husband's death.
Too much sorrow can be a blight.
My corner must be swept tonight.

Comb

Not content
with furrowing
my lady's skull

you root out
buds of hair
which you chew
calmly between
your celluloid cud

audacious lover
in no way bothered
by a few
molars missing

Grandma's Advice

If you have a little pussy
then you must treat it right
stroke it every day
stroke it every night

if you want that little pussy
to curl up by the fire
then you must do
what that pussy require

if you want to hear
that little pussy purr
I'm telling you sir
you must stroke its fur

groom it with your comb
sometimes slow sometimes quick
and you must remember
to give that pussy a lick

if you treat little pussy
thoughtless and rash
then little pussy
might begin to scratch

but if you want little pussy
in a playful fashion
then lay it down nicely
on a little cushion

Different Paths

The slut
was generous with her slit.
No if no but.

But the hermit
would have no part of it.

Alas
he died of solitude
on a bed free of sin

She died surrounded
by a brood
of distant kith and kin.

White Wedding

At a white wedding of wanton Betty
she whispered to her groom
later I'll shower you in cuntfetti

For the Moment

Touching with eyes
where fingers fail
they penetrate warm interiors
of riveryearning blood

holding with care
the core of silence
in the palm of their eyes

becoming for the moment
the centre of their blood's web
till the spider of speech
is ready to return